MEN OF THE BIBLE

MEN OF THE BIBLE

The Stories of
JOSHUA,
GIDEON, AND
JONAH

RETOLD BY
CARINE MACKENZIE

A BIBLETIME GIFT COLLECTION

An Inspirational Press Book for Children

First Inspirational Press edition published in 1998.

Inspirational Press
A division of BBS Publishing Corporation
386 Park Avenue South
New York, NY 10016

Inspirational Press is a registered trademark of BBS Publishing Corporation.

Published by arrangement with Christian Focus Publications, Ltd.

Library of Congress Catalog Card Number: 98-72391

ISBN: 0-88486-214-3

Printed in Mexico

Joshua

THE BRAVE LEADER

The Story of Joshua
accurately retold from the Bible,
(from the book of Joshua), by
CARINE MACKENZIE

Long ago there was a brave young
soldier called Joshua who
belonged to the Israelite people.

The Israelites had been slaves in Egypt for a long time but were at last led away by Moses from their hard life. God looked after them as they traveled through the desert to the land of Canaan. He promised to give them this land.

God told them that they would have to conquer the people of Canaan and that He would help them to do that.

Joshua was a very useful and faithful helper to Moses in leading the Israelites to their new land.

When the Israelites came near to the land of Canaan, God told Moses to send twelve men to spy out the land. Joshua was chosen as one of these spies.

The twelve spies went into Canaan and found that it was a very good land.

They returned after forty days to tell Moses what they had seen.

They showed the huge bunch of grapes which they took back from Canaan. It was so big that two of them had to carry it between them on a long stick. They also carried back pomegranates and figs.

All the spies told Moses that the land was rich and prosperous; but ten of them also brought back a bad report saying that the people of the land were too strong and too many for the Israelites to conquer. The Israelites believed the bad report and were afraid.

Joshua and his friend Caleb did not agree with the other spies and said to the people, "The land is very, very good. If the Lord is pleased with us, He will bring us into this land. Do not be afraid. The Lord is with us."

The people did not want to listen
to Joshua and Caleb. They wanted
to throw stones at them to kill
them.

Although God was angry with the people for their wickedness, He forgave them; but He said that they were not to be allowed to go to Canaan at that time. They would have to wander in the desert for forty years.

Only Joshua and Caleb and those of the people who were under 20 years old at that time would be allowed to arrive at the promised land at last. The rest of the people would die in the desert.

The ten spies who gave the bad report died, but Joshua and Caleb kept fit and well.

The people sinned by not believing the Lord. If we do not believe what God says in His word, then we are sinning too.

Joshua continued to help Moses to lead the people during their forty years of traveling in the desert.

Near the end of their journey, God said to Moses, who was now very old, "Take Joshua in front of the priest and all the people, and tell them that he will be their leader when you die."

Soon after that Moses died, and God said to Joshua, "You must now lead the people over the River Jordan into the promised land of Canaan. I will give you this land. I will be with you and I will not fail you."

What a wonderful promise for Joshua and his people. With God on their side, all would be well.

God is the same today. He promises to be with those who trust Him.

Joshua obeyed God immediately. He gave orders to the officers, "Tell everyone to get food ready. We will soon cross over the River Jordan in to the land of Canaan. The people obeyed him.

Joshua sent two men to spy out the land, and especially the city of Jericho. These two spies went to Jericho and stayed in the house of a woman called Rahab.

The king of Jericho sent his soldiers to Rahab's house to look for the spies, but Rahab had hidden them under stalks of flax on the flat roof of her house. She sent the soldiers away to look for the spies somewhere else.

She said to the spies, "When you come to capture our land, please be kind to me and my family because I was kind to you."
"Do not say a word to anyone about our business," replied the spies, "and we will be kind to you."

Rahab's house was on the town wall. She helped the spies escape down a scarlet rope from her window to the ground outside the town.

Before the men hurried away they said to Rahab, "When we come back to take the city, tie this scarlet rope in the window as a sign. All the people in the house with you will then be quite safe."

The men returned to Joshua and told him, "The Lord has really given us the land. All the people are very afraid of us."

So Joshua and the people rose early in the morning and went to the bank of the River Jordan. God told Joshua exactly what to do and Joshua passed on these orders to the people.

The priests went in front carrying the very special holy box called "the ark of the convenant of the Lord." The people followed behind at a distance.

As soon as the priests' feet stepped into the River Jordan, the water flowing down the river bed stopped and a big wall of water built up.

The priests stood still in the middle
of the river bed, which was now
dry, and the people were able to
walk over in safety, into the land of
Canaan. What an amazing miracle
God had done for His own people.

Joshua then built a pillar of twelve stones on the river bed where the priests had been standing. He also ordered twelve men to take a stone each from the river bed and carry them to Gilgal, their next camp site nearby. There they had to build another pillar. Joshua said to the people, "When your children ask what these stones mean, tell them how God stopped the River Jordan flowing, so that we could pass over safely."

We should remember how good God is to us and tell others about it.

When the priests carrying the ark
of the covenant moved on to the
other bank of the river, the River
Jordan flowed down as before.

Then the Israelites set up camp at
Gilgal, not very far from the city of
Jericho.

Joshua and the people were now
ready to begin conquering the land
of Canaan.

The people of Jericho knew that
the Israelites were on their way to
conquer the land. They were so
afraid that they closed the city
gates and stayed inside.

God told Joshua how he must capture their city. Joshua did exactly as God said and told the people what to do.

For six days the people marched once each day, round the walls of the city as God had said.

Soldiers led the way, followed by seven priests each blowing a trumpet. Then came more priests carrying the ark of the covenant. They were followed by the rest of the soldiers. Joshua told the people, "Do not make any noise at all until I tell you to shout."

On the seventh day they marched round the city, not just once but seven times. On the seventh time round, Joshua told the people, "Shout; for God has given you the city."

When the people shouted and the trumpets blew, the walls of Jericho fell down flat. The Israelites went straight into the city and destroyed it.

Joshua did not forget Rahab and
her kindness to the spies. He sent
the two spies to her house where
they saw the scarlet rope. She and
her family were saved alive.

The people were told that all the silver and gold and valuable things in Jericho belonged to the Lord. One man, Achan, stole some of this silver and gold and clothes for himself.

He hid them in the ground tent. But God had had done.

God sees everything we do.
Nothing that we say, or do, or think
is hidden from Him.

Achan's wickedness brought much
trouble to Israel, as we shall soon
see.

The next city that Joshua was to conquer was Ai. The Israelites thought that it would be quite easy to conquer this city but they got a terrible surprise. The men of Ai won the battle and chased them away.

Joshua was very upset about this defeat and he asked God why they had lost the battle. God told him that someone in the camp had sinned by stealing some of the precious things which belonged to the Lord.

Joshua rose early in the morning and God guided him to find out that Achan was the man in the camp who had sinned in this way.

Achan was severely punished. The people threw stones at him until he died. Achan died because of his sin.

The Lord told Joshua to go again to capture the city of Ai. This time they were successful.

After the battle the people worshipped God at Mount Ebal. Joshua read the whole law of God to all the people, young and old.

It is important for you also to know what God's commands are. Jesus tells us to love the Lord our God with all our heart, and with all our soul and with all our strength and with all our mind.

He also tells us to love other people as much as we love ourselves. We can keep these commands only with the help of the Lord Himself.

Joshua led the armies of Israel to many victories after that, because God fought for them. So in the end the Israelites won the whole land of Canaan. Then there was peace throughout the land.

Joshua had another important work to do. He had to divide the land of Canaan into parts so that each tribe of the Israelites had its own part to live in. Joshua was given his own special part: a city called Trimnath-serah.

When Joshua was very old, he called all the chief men of Israel together and gave them some good advice. "I am very old," he said. "You have seen all that the Lord God has done to give you this land. Take care to love the Lord God and to obey Him."

"You must serve the Lord alone," he urged them, "Choose this day whom you will serve, but as for me and my family, we will serve the Lord."

The people replied to Joshua, "We will serve the Lord, and obey Him."

If you had been there then, what would your reply have been?

Would you have said, "I will serve the Lord and obey Him?"

Ask the Lord to give you His love in your heart so that you will love to serve Him and obey His word, as Joshua did.

Joshua died at the great age of one hundred and ten years and was buried in his own part of the land.

Joshua had been a faithful servant of the Lord. God had been with him all the time, as He had promised, and so Joshua had been able to serve the Lord as the brave leader of God's people.

Gideon

SOLDIER OF GOD

The Story of Gideon
accurately retold from the Bible by
CARINE MACKENZIE

Long ago a man called Gideon
lived in the land of Israel. At that
time there was trouble in his land.

Enemies from the land of Midian raided the farms. They took away the sheep and cattle and stole the corn and grapes.

The people of Israel were frightened.

They prayed to God to help them.

We too can pray to God to ask Him to help us when we are in trouble. God can answer our prayers in surprising ways.

But what would happen to the people of Israel? How could God help them?

God had a plan to save His people.

One day Gideon was preparing some food. He was hiding behind a wine press so that none of the Midianite soldiers would see him and come to steal his food.

An angel of God came and sat down under an oak tree near where Gideon was working, but Gideon did not know that this stranger was an angel.

"God has chosen you, Gideon, to save your country from the Midianites," said the angel. Gideon was very surprised.

"How shall I save Israel?" he asked. "My family is poor and I am not great and important."

Then Gideon said to the angel, "Please do not go away. Wait there until I make some food for you."

So he fetched bread and meat in a basket and a pot of broth and took them back to the angel under the oak tree.

"Put the food on this rock," the angel told Gideon, "and then pour out the broth."

Gideon did as he was told. Then the angel touched the food with the end of his stick and what do you think happened?

Fire rose up out of the rock and burnt up the food completely. Then the angel of the Lord disappeared.

Gideon now knew that he had
been talking with an angel of God,
and he was afraid.

God is very holy. Gideon had done
many wrong things just like us.
This is why he was afraid.

But God said to him, "Do not be
afraid."

Gideon then built an altar so that
he could worship God there.

You know you can worship God in church. But did you know that you can worship Him at home or even in the playground?

One way to worship God is to pray from the heart and you can do that wherever you are.

The people in Israel at the time worshiped an idol named Baal in places called groves. This made God very angry. God told Gideon to destroy one of these groves.

So with the help of ten of his servants he cut it down and burnt it.

Gideon worshiped the only true God.

The Bible tells us to worship God only, and to put Him first in our lives.

We do not worship idols like Baal, but we sin every day when we do what pleases ourselves instead of what pleases God.

The angel had told Gideon that he
was to save his country from the
Midianites but Gideon was not
sure. He wanted to be certain.

So he asked God to do something
special for him.

He took a sheep's woolen coat, called a fleece, and put it outside on the ground one night. Gideon then prayed to God and asked Him to make the fleece wet with dew but to leave the ground round about it quite dry. If such a wonderful thing happened Gideon would be really sure that he was the man that God had chosen.

What would Gideon find in the morning?

As soon as it was daylight Gideon went out to see if his prayer had been answered. Yes it had! The ground was quite dry but the fleece was wet with dew—so wet that Gideon squeezed out a whole bowlful of water from it.

Was that not a wonderful answer
to his prayer?

Surely Gideon would now show
faith in God by obeying His
command!

No, not quite yet!

Again he prayed to God and said,
"Oh Lord, do not be angry with
me. I am still not sure. Please give
me one more sign. Let the fleece
be dry but the ground around it
wet with dew."

When Gideon went out next
morning to look at the fleece he
could doubt no longer. God had
again answered his prayer. The
ground was wet with dew but the
fleece was as dry as could be.

So Gideon was now quite sure that he would be the leader of Israel to save them from the people of Midian.

The Midianites had a large army in Israel.

Gideon also had a very big army of thirty-two thousand soldiers. God said to Gideon, "Your army is too big. If you beat the army of Midian with all these soldiers you will think that you did it by your own strength."

This time Gideon showed faith right away and said to his soldiers, "If any of you are afraid and want to go back home, just go."

So twenty-two thousand men went back home.

That left Gideon with ten thousand
men. Still too big an army!

God said to Gideon, "Take the
men down to the river to drink and
I will show you which ones to keep."

Most of the men drank by going
down on their knees and putting
their mouths right down into the
water.

God told Gideon to send these
men home.

Others drank by putting their
hands down into the river,
scooping up the water and lapping
it from their hands. There were
only three hundred men who did
this and God told Gideon to keep
these men as his helpers.

What a small army compared to
the thousands of soldiers in the
enemy camp. But this army had
God on its side.

We will soon see what a difference
that made.

That night God told Gideon to go down secretly to the enemy camp. He took his servant Phurah with him for company and they crept down in the darkness.

They stopped outside one of the tents when they overheard voices. One man was speaking to his friend. "I have just had a strange dream," he said, "A loaf of barley bread tumbled down into the camp and knocked over one of the tents. I wonder what it means."

His friend replied, "I know what it means! God is going to help Gideon to defeat us."

Gideon was encouraged when he overheard this conversation and he worshipped the Lord.

Gideon then got ready for battle.
He divided his three hundred men
into three groups.

Each group was to approach the
enemy from a different direction.

Every soldier had a trumpet and a lamp covered with an earthenware jug to hide the light. Gideon told them to watch him closely and do just as he did. When he would blow his trumpet, they had to do the same and shout loudly, "THE SWORD OF THE LORD AND OF GIDEON."

In the middle of the night, Gideon and his followers marched down towards the enemy camp.

All eyes were on Gideon. When would he give the sign?

Suddenly Gideon blew his trumpet.

They all blew their trumpets too. They also smashed the jugs so that the lamps shone brightly in the darkness.

They shouted as loudly as they could, "THE SWORD OF THE LORD AND OF GIDEON."

The enemy soldiers were terrified when they heard the noise and saw the lights roundabout. They ran this way and that in the darkness and started fighting with each other.

Then they took to their heels and ran away in panic.

Gideon and his men chased them right out of their land.

God had saved the people of Israel by using Gideon and a few soldiers.

After the victory the people of Israel said to Gideon, "Will you be our king and rule over us?"

Gideon replied, "No, the Lord will rule over you."

God is still ruling!

He is ruling in heaven, and He is ruling over everyone.

He always has done.

He always will.

For he is, "the same yesterday and today and for ever."

Gideon was an ordinary man but yet he led his people to this great victory. How? Because God was on his side. God has power over everything and everyone. He does wonderful things for those who are helpless but who trust in Him.

JONAH
THE RUNAWAY PREACHER

The Story of Jonah
accurately retold from the Bible by
CARINE MACKENZIE

Jonah was a Hebrew man who lived in the land of Israel. He loved the Lord God.

One day God spoke to him, giving him a very important message. "Go to the great city of Nineveh. Tell the people there that I see their wickedness."

"I don't want to do that," Jonah said to himself. Although Jonah loved the Lord, he did not obey Him then. Instead of going where God told him, he headed off in the opposite direction and reached the port of Joppa on the Mediterranean Sea.

God gives us commands in His
Word, the Bible. Very often we are
like Jonah and do what we want
ourselves instead of what God
wants us to do. This disobedience
is displeasing to God.

At Joppa, Jonah found a boat ready
to sail across the sea to Tarshish.

Jonah paid the fare and boarded the ship. The ship set sail, with Jonah down below as one of the passengers. He thought he was escaping from God and the difficult duties that God was placing on him.

Jonah was soon to learn that no one can run away from God.

God was seeing Jonah in the ship too. God is seeing us wherever we are. He sees us at home, at school, in the street. He still sees us when we are in a place where we ought not to be.

God, who is in charge of all weather conditions, sent a violent storm on the sea. The storm was so wild that it seemed that the ship would soon be broken up.

The sailors were scared. They threw the cargo overboard in order to make the boat lighter. That did no good. They were very worried. They prayed to their own false gods but of course they could not hear them. Only God, the Lord, can hear and answer prayer.

Through all the commotion, Jonah was fast asleep down below in the sides of the ship.

The captain came down and shook him awake. "What do you think you are doing, sleepy head? Get up and pray to your God. Perhaps He will save us from perishing," he said.

"Why has this disaster happened to us?" one man asked. "Who knows?" answered another. "Let's draw lots and see who the blame will fall on."

So they cast lots and it so happened that the lot fell on Jonah and
so he got the blame. This was not
decided by chance but by God
directing the whole matter.

The other men immediately pounced on Jonah. "You are to blame! Tell us why! What do you do? Where do you come from?" The questions flew from every side.

Jonah told them, "I am a Hebrew. I worship the Lord, the God of Heaven who made the sea and dry land. I am trying to run away from the presence of the Lord God," he added.

The men were very afraid. "Oh, why have you done this?" they moaned.

Even these heathen men realized that Jonah had done wrong, but the sea was getting rougher and rougher.

"What will we do to you, so that the sea would be made calm again?" they asked him.

Jonah's solution was very drastic. "Take me and throw me overboard into the sea. The sea will then be calm. This is all my fault," he said.

The men were reluctant to throw Jonah into the sea. They rowed as hard as they could in the direction of the land but with no success. No matter how hard they rowed they could make no headway and the sea grew even wilder than before.

These men, in desperation, cried in prayer to the Lord God. "O Lord, please do not let us die because of this man Jonah. Do not blame us. You, O Lord, have done just what pleases You."

With these words they caught
Jonah and threw him into the raging
sea. Down, down went Jonah into
the deep.

The sailors on board the ship were astounded. The moment Jonah hit the water, the sea became calm.

These men saw the power of the true God. They saw His control over the wind and the sea. They worshipped God there and then on the deck of the ship.

We can see God's power every day in the world around us. This should make us worship and praise Him.

What had happened to Jonah? Was that the end of him? No. God still had work for him to do.

God made all animals and fishes and has them in His control. God had arranged that a great big whale would swallow Jonah.

For three days and three nights Jonah lived inside the whale. He had air to breathe and so was saved from drowning.

Jonah was in great trouble. He cried to God in prayer while he was in the stomach of the whale.

"I cried to God because of my trouble and He heard me. You have brought me into great trouble in the depths of the sea. When my soul was fainting, I remembered the Lord. I prayed to You. Salvation is of the Lord."

Jonah worshipped God, confessed his wrong doing and thanked Him for His goodness in saving him.

God spoke to the whale and it vomited Jonah on to the dry land.

Jonah had another opportunity to obey God's voice. God spoke to him a second time. "Go to the great city of Nineveh and preach to the people whatever I tell you."

So Jonah went to Nineveh, a long way to the east. Nineveh was a huge place. Jonah entered the gates of the city and walked in towards the center. He was here to preach the Word of the Lord. He had been reluctant to go at first but now he was not going to shirk his duty.

His message was loud and clear.
"In forty days time the city of
Nineveh shall be destroyed," he
proclaimed.

The people of Nineveh heard Jonah's words and they believed God. They were so sorry for their sins that they stopped eating food. They dressed in rough sackcloth. Even the King took off his beautiful robe and wore sackcloth like every-one else. He did not sit on his throne. Instead he sat on the ground, in the ashes.

The King sent an order through the city. "We must all cry to God. We must all turn from our evil ways," he said. "We must stop violence. Perhaps God will not destroy us after all."

God took notice of the people of Nineveh. He heard their cries and He saw that they were truly sorry for their sins.

So God decided not to destroy the people of Nineveh.

Because of Jonah's message, many people were changed and served the true God. How pleased Jonah ought to have been. He had been used by God in converting many souls.

But Jonah was very angry. He was
not at all pleased.

"This is just what I thought would happen," he told God. "I knew You were a gracious, merciful God. I knew You were very kind and would not destroy those people at all. That is why I decided to run away to Tarshish."

Jonah was afraid that he would look foolish if his prophesies of destruction did not happen.

"Take my life away," he said to God. "It is better for me to die."
"Do you think you are right to be so angry?" God asked him.

God then taught Jonah another lesson.

Jonah left the city in a bad mood. He climbed up on the east side of the town to a place where he would get a good view of all that was happening. He made a little shelter for himself and sat down to wait.

God, who has all plants in His control, made a creeping plant, with big leaves, to grow up. This gave very welcome shade to Jonah. He was very glad to sit under it in the heat of the day.

God has all the creeping animals in His control too. Next day God sent a worm to gnaw at the roots of the plant. The plant withered and died. No more cool shade for Jonah.

God, who is in charge of the winds, sent a very hot east wind. Jonah became hotter and hotter—so hot that he felt faint and very depressed. "It would be better if I was dead," he said to himself.

"Do you think you are right to be angry because the plant was destroyed?" God asked him.

"Of course I am right to be angry about that," replied Jonah. "You are sorry for that plant which you have not planted or tended. Should you not have as much pity for that great city of Nineveh as you have for a poor plant that grew in one night?" God replied.

Jonah himself had been wonderfully spared from destruction. He had been shown mercy. How he should have rejoiced that God showed mercy to thousands of people in Nineveh.

God's mercy is still being shown to sinners today. God's mercies are new every morning. We are told to "Seek the Lord while He may be found, call upon Him while He is near. Let the wicked forsake his way and the unrighteous man his thoughts and let him return unto the Lord and He will have mercy upon him."

The Lord Jesus speaks about Jonah. He compares Himself to Jonah. Jesus said that He would be three days and nights in the grave.

The Lord Jesus suffered this humiliation and suffering of death so that those who trust in Him would have everlasting life.